History Of Korea For Kids
A History Series
Children Explore Histories Of The World Edition

SPEEDY
PUBLISHING

Speedy Publishing LLC
40 E. Main St. #1156
Newark, DE 19711
www.speedypublishing.com

At first Korea was divided into tribes but eventually organised kingdoms emerged.

China tried
to defeat the
northern kingdom
of Goguryeo
twice.

Then, the Chinese then made an alliance with the Silla kingdom against the other two.

The Baekje kingdom was defeated by 660 AD and became part of Silla. Goguryeo followed in 668. Korea was then united under the Silla.

Korean society
was strictly
hierarchical.

Most of the population were serfs and even the nobility were divided into ranks.

Buddhism was introduced into Korea in the 4th century AD and soon many Buddhist temples were built.

In the late 8th century AD the Silla kingdom began to break down. There were fights over the succession to the throne.

During the 19th century Korea adopted an isolationist policy. The Koreans refused to trade with Westerners.

In 1910, the Japanese turned Korea into a colony to supply Japan with food.

From 1938 education was only in Japanese. Schoolchildren were forbidden to speak Korean.

Japanese attempts to turn Korea into part of Japan were ended in 1945 when they surrendered to the allies.

In August 1945 Russian troops entered the north. In September, after the Japanese surrender, American troops landed in the south.

The Russians installed a communist government in the north and in the south a government was elected in 1948. Korea became two countries, one Communist, and one Democratic.

In 2013 the people of North Korea still face terrible hardship and even starvation as well as brutal political oppression.

The Korean History is very interesting, research and learn more!

Made in the USA
Middletown, DE
31 August 2017